WEALTH BY DESIGN

From Income to Impact

A Practical Guide to Wealth Creation, Financial Freedom, and Lasting Legacy

Augusta Olachi Anyanwu-Egbom

"Create so much value that money has no choice but to follow you."

...a Wealth Mentor Philosophy
Augusta Olachi Anyanwu-Egbom

WEALTH BY DESIGN: From Income to Impact

ISBN: 978-978-68-9752-3

First Edition: August 2026

Published by: Storyteller Services, Lagos, Nigeria
info@storyteller-services.com
www.storyteller-services.com
+234 815 655 5108

Wealth by Design is a publication of the Wealth Mentor Platform, advancing the nation-building mission of The Duke's Infant & Child Foundation (TDIC Foundation)
www.tdicfoundation.org/wealthbydesign
+2348023319710 / +447480539285

Printed in Nigeria.

Dedication

This book is dedicated to everyone who believes that wealth is more than money; that impact is greater than income; and that true success is measured not only by what we accumulate, but by what we create, contribute, and leave behind.

To the loving memory of my parents, Mr. Julian and Mrs. Rufina Anyanwu, for their sacrifices, values, and unwavering belief in my potential planted seeds they did not live long enough to see fully bloom. Everything I continue to build carries the imprint of what you first deposited in me. Your legacy lives on through every page of this book.

To my remarkable son, David-Duke NkwaChimemeela Egbom, an imaginative creator and emerging best-selling young author, whose six published books before the age of ten challenged me to match his courage before stepping onto the fifth floor of my life. My son, I accepted your challenge; this book is proof that inspiration knows no age. Thank you for reminding me that dreams should never be postponed.

To my precious daughter, Keona, whose innocent heart and joyful reminders about making a real difference continually call me back to what matters most. You represent the future we are building today, and the legacy we hope to leave behind.

And to every dreamer, builder, entrepreneur, professional, parent, and change-maker who desires to create wealth with purpose and leave the world better than they found it, this book was written with you in mind. May it inspire you to intentionally design a life of freedom, significance, and lasting legacy.

Contents

Acknowledgements
Introduction .... *xi*

PART ONE: THE FOUNDATION OF WEALTH

Chapter One: Defining True Wealth 2
What Is Wealth? 3
The Four Dimensions of Wealth 3
What Is True Wealth? 4
The Wealth Illusion 6

Chapter Two: The Psychology of Financial Success 11
The Invisible Money Script 12
The Scarcity Vs Abundance Mindset 13
The Success Habits of Wealth Builders 17

Chapter Three: Financial Planning for Life 20
What Is A Financial Plan? 21
Why Most People Fail Financially 21
The Power of Written Goals 26

PART TWO: MASTERING YOUR MONEY

Chapter Four: Money Management Essentials 31
The Purpose of Money Management 32
The Five Destinations of Every Naira 33
The C.A.S.H. System 34

Chapter Five: The Wealth-Building Formula 42
The G.R.O.W. Formula 44
The Power of Compounding 47

The Enemy of Wealth 47

Chapter Six: Investing For Growth and Security 51

Why Investing Matters 52

The Difference Between Saving and Investing 53

The P.L.A.N.T. Framework 53

Biggest Investment Mistakes 57

PART THREE: EXPANDING YOUR WEALTH

Chapter Seven: The Power of Multiple Income Streams 62

What Is An Income Stream? 64

The Difference Between Active and Passive Income 64

The B.U.I.L.D. Framework 65

Chapter Eight: Creating Value Before Seeking Profit 72

Why Value Always Wins 75

The V.A.L.U.E. Framework 75

The Law of Exchange 77

Chapter Nine: Entrepreneurship and Economic Empowerment 82

The Entrepreneurial Mindset 84

The C.R.E.A.T.E. Framework™ 85

The Biggest Entrepreneurial Mistakes 89

PART FOUR: PROTECTING AND MULTIPLYING WEALTH

Chapter Ten: Financial Wisdom for Sustainable Impact 93

The Difference Between Knowledge and Wisdom 95

The S.T.E.W.A.R.D. Framework™ 96

Chapter Eleven: Wealth Preservation Strategies 102

What Threatens Wealth? 104

The P.R.O.T.E.C.T. Framework™ 105

PART FIVE: FROM WEALTH TO LEGACY

Chapter Twelve: Building Generational Wealth and Legacy 113

What Is Generational Wealth? 115

The Five Pillars of Generational Wealth 116

The L.E.G.A.C.Y. Framework™ 117

Conclusion 126

Acknowledgements

Every meaningful journey and experience is shaped by people whose contributions are sometimes visible but more often invisible. *Wealth by Design* is no exception. First and foremost, I give all glory to God, the Author of wisdom and the Giver of every good gift. Thank You for the grace to learn, to lead, to serve, and now, to write. This book is another expression of Your faithfulness in my life.

To my family, thank you for your love, your patience, and for graciously sharing me with the many responsibilities and assignments that have shaped my life. Your support has been one of my greatest strengths.

To Fidelity Bank Plc, where I have been privileged to serve for well over a decade and a half at the time of writing this book, thank you for giving me wings to grow. Beyond a career, the institution provided an environment that sharpened my leadership, expanded my financial knowledge, and nurtured the intrapreneurial spirit that deepened my understanding of wealth creation, stewardship, and financial freedom, both in principle and in practice. Many of the lessons captured in these pages were refined through years of serving clients, supporting entrepreneurs, building businesses, and creating value within this remarkable institution.

To Engr. Nnamdi Ezigbo, founder of Slot Systems Limited, thank you for an encounter many years ago that brought our paths together and created an opportunity. That single opportunity opened doors to ventures that broadened my understanding of enterprise, strengthened my conviction in building multiple streams of value, and, by God's grace, created employment and opportunities for many other families. Thank you for demonstrating that one opportunity, embraced with vision, diligence, and purpose, can multiply its impact far beyond the person who first receives it.

To Emmanuel Ukwadiachi, thank you for being much more than a digital support. Over the years, you developed a rare ability to distill my financial wisdom into simple, compelling creatives that uniquely echoed my voice with very little direction. Through the *Wealth Marbles*, content calendars, and countless creative pieces we developed together, you helped make timeless principles accessible to thousands. Even the moments that required us to rethink, refine, or begin again became part of the creative journey that ultimately helped shape the direction and purpose of this book. Thank you for staying the course.

To the countless individuals whose names I may never know, yet whose words have remained with me—those who quietly stopped me after church to say, *"Your posts have helped me,"* or *"Please don't stop writing"*; to colleagues who mentioned, often in passing, how a Wealth Mentor post changed their perspective, influenced a financial decision, or arrived at exactly the right moment—thank you.

Many of you never left a comment. Many never clicked "Like." Many never shared a post. Yet your quiet encouragement reminded me that impact is not always measured by visible engagement. Sometimes, the deepest transformations happen in silence.

To every mentor, leader, colleague, client, entrepreneur, educator, and friend who knowingly or unknowingly became part of my journey, thank you. Every conversation, every challenge, every success, every disappointment, and every lesson has found its way into these pages.

Finally, to every reader who chose to pick up this book, thank you for trusting me with your time and attention. In a world overflowing with information, you chose to invest in wisdom, and I do not take that lightly.

If these pages inspire you to think differently, steward wisely, create greater value, and build a legacy that outlives you, then every lesson, every experience, every sacrifice, and every late night invested in writing this book will have been worthwhile.

Thank you for becoming part of the *Wealth by Design* story.

Our journey is only just beginning.

Introduction

Before you begin reading, there is something I would like you to know.

This is not just another personal finance book. It is not a collection of motivational quotes, a promise of overnight wealth or a shortcut to financial success.

This book is an invitation to intentionally design a life of financial freedom, meaningful impact, and lasting legacy.

For close to three decades, I have had the privilege of sitting at tables where life-changing financial decisions were made. Through my career in banking, I have worked with individuals, entrepreneurs, businesses, and institutions to unlock opportunities, finance dreams, build enterprises, preserve wealth, and create value measured not merely in millions but in billions.

Those experiences have taught me one profound truth: money is powerful, but wisdom is priceless.

Over the years, I have seen people with very little build extraordinary wealth through discipline, sound values, and intentional decisions.

I have also seen people with extraordinary resources lose almost everything because they lacked the wisdom to steward what they had.

Those experiences changed me.

They taught me that wealth is never an accident; it is intentionally designed.

Some people assume this book was written because I have accumulated enormous personal wealth. The truth is different.

I am not writing this book because I consider myself a billionaire by the balance in my bank account. I am writing it because I have come to understand the immense value that knowledge, wisdom, experience, and purpose can create in the lives of others.

If there is one form of wealth I deeply cherish, it is the privilege of helping people see possibilities they never imagined, make decisions that transform their future, and build lives that create opportunities for generations to come. To me, that is wealth: significance, and fulfilment.

As I reflected on the journey that has shaped my life, I realised something deeply concerning: we are raising a generation with unprecedented access to information and knowledge but limited access to timeless financial wisdom.

Many young people know how to earn money but have never been taught how to manage it. They aspire to success but have not been shown the disciplines that sustain it. They admire lifestyles but rarely understand the values that created them. They pursue income without first discovering purpose. Yet the future of every nation is shaped by the financial decisions of its people. That burden has remained in my heart for years. It is one of the reasons this book exists.

Through my Wealth Mentor platform, I have spent years sharing lessons on money, value creation, entrepreneurship, investing, leadership, stewardship, and legacy. Those conversations have reached thousands of people and have convinced me that what many people truly need is not another formula for getting rich. They need wisdom, direction, and principles that stand the test of time.

This book brings together those lessons into one practical journey: a journey from Income to Impact.

Unlike many books that simply tell you what to do, Wealth by Design is written to help you think differently, decide wisely, and act intentionally. Each chapter is carefully structured to move you from understanding wealth to building it.

Inside these pages you will find:

- Wealth Marbles (Timeless principles that capture the heart of each chapter.)

- Wealth Mentor's Notes (Personal reflections from my own journey.)
- Practical Frameworks (Simple systems that transform ideas into action.)
- Real-Life Case Studies (Relatable examples that bring financial principles to life.)
- Wealth Worksheets (Practical exercises to personalise your learning.)
- Wealth Checkpoints (Opportunities to measure your progress.)
- Wealth Challenges (Action steps that turn knowledge into lasting habits.)

Please don't simply read this book.
Write in it.
Reflect on it.
Discuss it.
Challenge yourself with it.

Return to it often because information informs, but application transforms.

This is one of the most meaningful works of my life because I believe impact has a multiplier effect. Beyond my professional career, I have dedicated my life to raising leaders, mentoring individuals, strengthening families, and building communities through financial education, leadership development, and social impact initiatives.

Every life transformed has reinforced one conviction: when one person learns to build wealth with wisdom, an entire family can change.

When families change, communities become stronger.

When communities become stronger, nations prosper.

That is why I believe financial wisdom is more than personal success, it is nation-building.

So, as you turn these pages, I invite you to journey with me.

Question old beliefs.
Challenge familiar habits.
Create more value than you consume.
Build wealth with integrity.
Steward it with wisdom.
Use it with purpose.

Leave a legacy that continues speaking long after you are gone.
Above all, remember this: wealth is never an accident; it is intentionally designed.

Welcome to the journey. Let's begin.

Part One

THE FOUNDATION OF WEALTH

Chapter One
Defining True Wealth

Wealth Marble

Money can buy comfort, but only wisdom can create wealth. Wealth is not measured by what you spend today, but by the freedom, choices, and impact your resources create tomorrow.

Most people spend years chasing money without ever stopping to define wealth.

Ask a young graduate what wealth means, and they might answer by saying:

A luxury car.
A mansion.
A six-figure salary.
Designer brands.
First-class travel.

These things may be enjoyable, but they are not wealth.

Many people look wealthy while living pay cheque to pay cheque.

Others appear ordinary while quietly building assets, investments, businesses, and financial freedom.

The danger is obvious: when you misunderstand wealth, you pursue the wrong goals and when you pursue the wrong goals, you may arrive at a destination you never wanted.

The first step towards financial freedom is understanding what wealth truly is.

What Is Wealth?

Wealth is not income.
Wealth is not possessions.
Wealth is not status.

Wealth is the ability to live life on your own terms without being controlled by financial pressure or influence. Wealth gives you options, choices, peace, attention, and significant capacity to create lasting impact.

The Four Dimensions of Wealth

Many people focus only on financial wealth. Successful people understand there are four dimensions.

1. Financial Wealth

Your assets exceed your liabilities.
You have investments.

You have savings.

You have income-producing assets.

Money is working for you, not the other way around.

2. Time Wealth

You control your schedule.

You are not trapped.

You can spend time where it matters most.

Many people have money but no time.

That is not freedom.

3. Relationship Wealth

Your network matters.

Trust matters.

Character matters.

Your reputation is an invisible asset.

One relationship can change your life.

One broken relationship can cost you opportunities.

4. Legacy Wealth

What remains after you're gone?

What values have you transferred?

What systems have you built?

What impact have you created?

It is important to always remember that the highest level of wealth is legacy.

What Is True Wealth?

Most people spend their lives pursuing money without ever defining wealth.

Ask ten people what it means to be wealthy and many will describe expensive cars, luxury homes, designer brands, or large bank accounts.

Society has conditioned us to associate wealth with visible possessions. Yet some of the wealthiest-looking people are financially trapped, while some of the truly wealthy live with remarkable simplicity.

The problem is not that people want wealth.

The problem is that many are chasing symbols instead of substance.

A person earning millions can still be financially stressed. Another earning far less may enjoy peace, security, freedom, and purpose because they understand principles that money alone cannot buy.

True wealth is bigger than income.

It is the ability to live life on your own terms, provide for those you love, withstand financial shocks, pursue meaningful opportunities, and leave something valuable behind for future generations.

Wealth creates options. It gives you the freedom to make decisions based on purpose rather than desperation. It allows you to pursue opportunities instead of merely surviving and provides the capacity to help others without becoming a burden yourself.

One of the greatest misconceptions of our generation is believing that increasing income automatically creates wealth.

It does not.

Many people have increased their income without improving their financial position because wealth is not determined by what comes in.

Wealth is determined by what remains, what grows, and what continues working when you are no longer working.

Income pays bills.

Wealth creates freedom.

Income can disappear next month but wealth continues producing value long after the original effort has ended.

This distinction is critical because many people spend years working for money while very little of that money ever works for them.

The journey to financial freedom begins when we stop asking, *"How much money can I make?"* and start asking:

"How can I build assets, create value, and intentionally design a life of lasting financial freedom?"

That is the difference between earning an income and building wealth and that difference can change the trajectory of an individual, a family, and generations yet unborn.

The Wealth Illusion

Social media has created a dangerous illusion.

People now compare lifestyles rather than balance sheets.

Someone may appear rich online, yet be drowning in debt.

Another person may appear ordinary, yet own businesses, investments, properties, and financial assets.

Never confuse visibility with wealth.

Framework #1: The Wealth Pyramid

Level 1: Survival

- Living pay cheque to pay cheque

- Constant financial stress
- No savings

Level 2: Stability

- Budgeting
- Emergency fund
- Basic financial discipline

Level 3: Security

- Investments
- Insurance
- Asset ownership

Level 4: Freedom

- Passive income
- Multiple income streams
- Financial independence

Level 5: Legacy

- Wealth transfer
- Family impact
- Philanthropy
- Nation building

The goal is not merely income, the goal is progression.

The Difference Between Income and Wealth

A doctor earns ₦2 million monthly while a business owner earns ₦500,000 monthly.

The doctor spends everything.

The entrepreneur invests 30%.

Ten years later, the doctor remains dependent on monthly income while the entrepreneur owns assets.

Who is wealthier?

Always remember that income creates opportunity and wealth creates freedom.

Framework #2: The Wealth Formula

Income + Savings + Investments + Time + Discipline = Wealth

Miss any component and wealth becomes difficult.

Why Young People Must Understand This Early

One of the greatest advantages of wealth creation is time.

A 25-year-old investing consistently can outperform a 45-year-old earning three times as much.

Time multiplies money. Delay destroys opportunity.

The earlier you begin, the easier wealth creation becomes.

Practical Exercise

Complete the following:

- My Current Monthly Income: ____________________
- My Monthly Expenses: ____________________

- My Monthly Savings: ____________________
- My Investments: ____________________
- My Debts: ____________________
- My Net Worth: ____________________

Most people have never calculated these numbers; yet they want financial freedom.

You cannot improve what you do not measure.

Wealth Mentor Framework

The D.E.S.I.G.N Model

D – Define what wealth means to you
E – Evaluate your current position
S – Set clear financial goals
I – Invest consistently
G – Grow your knowledge
N – Never stop creating value

This is how wealth is designed.

Not by luck.

Not by wishes.

Not by social media appearances.

By intention.

Reflection Questions

- What does wealth mean to me?
- Am I building assets or merely increasing expenses?
- What is my biggest financial habit?
- What wealth level am I currently on?
- What changes must I make this year?

Wealth Challenge

For the next 30 days:

✓ Track every naira.

✓ Record every expense.

✓ Calculate your net worth.

✓ Identify one asset you can begin building.

✓ Write your personal definition of wealth.

Because the journey to financial freedom begins with clarity.

Like any meaningful achievement, wealth is first designed before it is built.

Chapter Two

The Psychology of Financial Success

Wealth Marble

Your financial future is first created in your mind before it appears in your bank account.

Why do two people with similar backgrounds, education, and opportunities end up with completely different financial outcomes?

Why does one person steadily build wealth while another repeatedly struggles despite earning a decent income? The answer is often not found in their salaries, but their psychology.

Long before wealth appears in your account, it begins in your thinking.

Every financial decision you make is influenced by what you believe about money.

Whether you realise it or not, your beliefs determine your behaviour.

Your behaviour determines your habits.

Your habits ultimately determine your financial outcomes.

This is why financial success is not merely a money issue. It is a mindset issue.

Most people are trying to change their financial results without first changing their financial thinking.

That is like trying to change the fruit while ignoring the roots.

If the roots remain unhealthy, the fruit will always reflect it.

The same principle applies to wealth creation.

To build lasting wealth, we must first understand the beliefs driving our financial decisions.

The Invisible Money Script

Every person grows up with a 'money script'. A money script is the collection of beliefs, experiences, observations, and emotions we develop about money from childhood.

Some people grew up hearing:

- *"Money is hard to make."*
- *"Rich people are greedy."*
- *"Wealth is only for the lucky."*
- *"People like us never become wealthy."*
- *"Money changes people."*

Others grew up hearing:

- *"Money is a tool."*

- *"Wealth is created through value."*
- *"Investing builds freedom."*
- *"Opportunities exist everywhere."*

These messages shape how we think long before we earn our first salary. Many adults are still operating from financial beliefs they never consciously examined.

The problem is that false beliefs produce limiting behaviours.

If you believe wealth is only for the privileged, you will never intentionally pursue it.

If you believe investing is dangerous, you may never invest.

If you believe financial success is selfish, you may unconsciously sabotage your own progress.

Your financial life often reflects the story you keep telling yourself.

The Scarcity Vs Abundance Mindset

One of the most important mental shifts in wealth creation is moving from scarcity thinking to abundance thinking.

Scarcity thinking says:

- *"There is not enough."*
- *"If someone wins, I lose."*
- *"Opportunities are limited."*
- *"I am already too late."*

Abundance thinking says:

- *"There is always room to create value."*
- *"There are opportunities everywhere."*
- *"Knowledge can create wealth."*
- *"I can learn, improve, and grow."*

People with scarcity thinking often make decisions out of fear.

People with abundance thinking make decisions based on possibilities.

This does not mean ignoring reality; it means refusing to allow fear to become your financial adviser.

Framework #1: The Wealth Mindset Model

Awareness → Belief → Decision → Action → Habit → Result

Every financial outcome begins with a belief.

Change the belief and you begin changing the result.

If you believe wealth creation is possible, seek knowledge.

When you seek knowledge, you make better decisions.

Better decisions create better habits.

Better habits create better outcomes.

The Comfort Zone Trap

Many people dream of financial freedom but remain trapped in financial comfort zones.

The comfort zone is not always comfortable. It is simply familiar.

Some people stay in jobs they have outgrown.

Some avoid investing because they fear losing money.

Others never start businesses because they fear failure.

Growth requires discomfort.

Every major financial breakthrough usually begins with a decision that feels uncomfortable at first.

The first investment.

The first business.

The first property.

The first difficult financial conversation.

The first step towards freedom is often the hardest.

The Role of Delayed Gratification

One of the strongest predictors of financial success is delayed gratification, the ability to sacrifice today's pleasure for tomorrow's reward.

We live in a generation that promotes instant everything.

Instant delivery.
Instant entertainment.

Instant recognition.
Instant gratification.

Unfortunately, wealth does not work that way.

Real wealth rewards patience.

The investor who stays committed.
The entrepreneur who remains consistent.
The professional who continuously develops valuable skills.
The individual who chooses assets over appearances.

Financial maturity begins when you stop asking:

"What do I want now?"

And start asking:

"What will this decision cost me five years from now?"

Framework #2: The Decision Filter

Before every significant financial decision, ask yourself the following:

- Is this a need or a want?
- Will this increase or decrease my future options?
- Does this align with my financial goals?
- Is this helping me build assets or liabilities?
- Will my future self thank me for this decision?

This simple filter can prevent thousands of poor financial choices.

The Power of Financial Identity

People act consistently with who they believe they are.

Someone who sees themselves as financially irresponsible behaves differently from someone who sees themselves as a disciplined wealth builder.

Instead of saying:

"I am bad with money."

Say:

"I am learning to manage money wisely."

Instead of saying:

"I can never invest."

Say:

"I am becoming an investor."

Identity influences behaviour, behaviour influences results.

The wealthiest transformation often begins with changing how you see yourself.

The Success Habits of Wealth Builders

Throughout history, financially successful people have displayed common habits:

- Continuous learning
- Long-term thinking
- Strategic planning
- Consistency

- Personal responsibility
- Calculated risk-taking
- Value creation

Notice that none of these requires extraordinary talent. They require intentionality.

Framework #3: The Mindset Shift Formula

- From Consumer → Creator
- From Employee Only → Wealth Builder
- From Spending First → Investing First
- From Scarcity → Abundance
- From Excuses → Ownership
- From Short-Term Thinking → Long-Term Vision

This shift changes everything.

Reflection Questions

- What money beliefs did I inherit growing up?
- Which financial belief is limiting my progress?
- Where am I operating from scarcity rather than abundance?
- What financial risks have I avoided because of fear?
- What identity must I adopt to become the person I want to be financially?

Wealth Challenge

For the next 21 days:

- ✓ Write down every negative belief you have about money.
- ✓ Replace each one with an empowering belief.
- ✓ Read one chapter of a financial book daily.
- ✓ Listen to one financial podcast weekly.
- ✓ Identify one financial action you have delayed and take the first step.

Remember:

Financial freedom is not built by luck. It is built by beliefs, decisions, habits, and discipline.

The wealth you desire begins with the mindset you develop.

Your financial future is first created in your mind before it appears in your bank account.

Chapter Three
Financial Planning for Life

Wealth Marble

If you don't design your financial future, life will design one for you and you may not like the outcome.

Imagine setting out on a journey from Lagos to Kigali without knowing the route, checking your fuel gauge, or deciding where you're headed.

It sounds reckless, yet millions of people live their financial lives exactly that way.

They wake up every day, earn an income, spend most of it, save whatever is left—if anything is left—and hope that somehow everything will work out.

Hope is a beautiful virtue.

But hope is not a financial strategy.

Money is a wonderful servant but a terrible master. Left without direction, it disappears. Given a clear assignment, it becomes one of the greatest tools for creating freedom, opportunities, and impact.

One of the greatest differences between financially successful people and those who struggle is not the size of their income.

It is that one group lives by financial design while the other lives by financial default.

Financial planning is simply giving your money a purpose before it arrives.

What Is a Financial Plan?

A financial plan is not merely a spreadsheet.

It is not a budget.

It is not a savings account.

A financial plan is a roadmap that connects today's decisions to tomorrow's dreams.

It answers five important questions:

- Where am I today?
- Where do I want to be?
- How will I get there?
- What resources do I need?
- How will I measure my progress?

Without these answers, even a high income can disappear without creating lasting wealth.

Why Most People Fail Financially

It is rarely because they don't earn enough. Most people fail because they:

- Spend before planning.
- Save without goals.
- Invest without knowledge.
- Borrow without strategy.
- Live for today while ignoring tomorrow.

Money follows direction.

Without direction, money follows emotion.

The Wealth Mentor Blueprint ™

The D.E.S.I.G.N. Framework

This framework is the heartbeat of Wealth by Design.

D – Define Your Vision

What kind of life do you want?

Not next month.

Not next year.

Ten years from now:

- Where will you live?
- What work will you be doing?
- How much passive income do you want?
- What legacy do you hope to leave?

If your destination is unclear, every road will seem acceptable.

E – Evaluate Your Current Position

You cannot build your future by ignoring your present.

Know your numbers.

- Monthly income
- Monthly expenses
- Savings
- Investments
- Debts
- Net worth

Many people know their favourite football team's statistics better than their own financial position.

Clarity creates confidence.

S – Set Smart Financial Goals

Dreams inspire.

Goals direct.

Turn vague ambitions into measurable targets.

Instead of saying:

"I want to save more."

Say:

"I will save ₦2,000,000 over the next 18 months by investing ₦111,000 monthly."

Specific goals produce specific actions.

I – Implement the Plan

Knowledge without execution changes nothing.

Start where you are.

Automate savings.

Pay yourself first.

Track expenses.

Review investments.

Consistency beats intensity.

G – Grow Your Wealth

Money should not remain idle. Every naira should have an assignment.

Some should protect you.

Some should grow.

Some should generate income.

Some should create opportunities.

The goal is not merely to earn money; the goal is to multiply it.

N – Never Stop Reviewing

Constantly review the important things in your life.

- Marriage
- Children
- Career changes
- Business
- Inflation
- Economic cycles

Your financial plan must evolve with your life.

Review your plan every quarter.

Review your goals every year.

Framework #1: The Wealth House

Imagine your financial life as a house.

Foundation

- Mindset
- Values
- Discipline

Pillars

- Income
- Savings
- Investments
- Protection

Roof

- Financial Freedom
- Legacy
- Impact

A weak foundation cannot support a strong roof.

The Power of Written Goals

Research consistently shows that people who write their goals are far more likely to achieve them.

Writing transforms wishes into commitments.

Your financial goals deserve to be written, reviewed, and refined.

Your future deserves that level of intentionality.

The 70-20-10 Guide (Starting Point)

For readers beginning their financial journey:

- 70% – Living Expenses
- 20% – Wealth Building
- 10% – Giving and Personal Development

This is not a rigid rule.

It is a starting framework that encourages intentional allocation rather than accidental spending.

As your income grows, increase the percentage allocated to investments rather than lifestyle inflation.

Framework #3: The Future Decision Filter

Before making any major purchase, ask yourself: will this purchase...

- Increase my income?
- Increase my assets?
- Improve my knowledge?
- Improve my productivity?
- Appreciate in value?
- Move me closer to financial freedom?

If the answer is "No" to most of these questions, reconsider the purchase.

Every financial decision either builds your future or delays it.

Case Study

Two friends graduate from university at age 25 and each earns ₦500,000 monthly.

Sarah creates a financial plan. She saves consistently, invests monthly, avoids unnecessary debt, and reviews her goals every year.

James has no plan. He spends impulsively, upgrades his lifestyle with every salary increase, and assumes he will "figure it out later."

At age 40, both have earned similar incomes.

Sarah owns investment assets, has multiple income streams, and enjoys financial security.

James is still dependent on his monthly salary.

The difference was never income.

The difference was intentional design.

Reflection Questions

- Have I written a financial plan?
- What are my financial goals for the next one, five, and ten years?
- What financial habits are helping me?
- Which habits are delaying my progress?
- What one decision can I make today that my future self will celebrate?

Wealth Challenge

Complete your personal financial blueprint. Write down:

✓ Your current net worth.

✓ Your monthly cash flow.

✓ Your five-year financial vision.

✓ Three assets you want to own.

✓ Your retirement target.

✓ Your legacy goal.

Then schedule a quarterly "Money Meeting" with yourself.

- Review your finances.
- Celebrate progress.
- Correct mistakes.
- Adjust your strategy.

Remember:

The future does not happen by accident.

It is designed.

And every great financial future begins with a written plan.

Part Two
MASTERING YOUR MONEY

Chapter Four

Money Management Essentials

Wealth Marble

Every naira or dollar without an assignment will eventually find a way to disappear.

Money is like water. If you don't channel it, it will find its own path.

Many people believe their financial problems would disappear if only they earned more money.

But history tells a different story.

Lottery winners have gone bankrupt.

Professional athletes have retired in financial distress.

Celebrities who earned millions have ended up in debt.

Why?

Because income does not create financial security. Good money management does.

One of the greatest misconceptions about wealth is believing that earning more automatically leads to having more.

It doesn't.

Many people experience what economists call **lifestyle inflation**. As their income increases, so do their expenses.

A salary increase leads to a bigger car.

A promotion leads to a bigger house.

A bonus leads to a more expensive lifestyle.

Soon, despite earning significantly more than before, they remain trapped in the same financial cycle.

Money management is not about restricting your life.

It is about directing your money towards the life you truly want.

If Chapter Three taught us how to design a financial plan, Chapter Four teaches us how to execute it every single day.

The Purpose of Money Management

Money management is the intentional process of directing every naira towards your priorities rather than allowing your emotions to decide where it goes.

Good money management gives you:

- Clarity
- Control
- Confidence

- Financial Peace

When you know where your money is going, you gain the confidence to make better decisions.

The Five Destinations of Every Naira

Every naira you earn has only five possible destinations:

1. Spend It

For daily living expenses.

- Food
- Transportation
- Utilities
- Lifestyle

2. Save It

- For emergencies
- Planned purchases
- Unexpected events

Savings create breathing space.

3. Invest It

To create future wealth.

Investments allow your money to work even while you sleep.

4. Give It

In this context, I remind us of tithes and offerings. Generosity develops gratitude.

Giving reminds us that wealth is a tool, not a master.

5. Waste It

Every financial decision that adds no lasting value falls into this category.

- Impulse buying
- Subscriptions you never use
- Status purchases.
- Emotional spending.

Money wasted today is opportunity lost tomorrow.

The Wealth Mentor Blueprint™

The C.A.S.H. System

Whenever money enters your account, pause and walk through the C.A.S.H. system before deciding how to use it.

C — Capture It

Know exactly how much came in.

Never guess your income.

Know your numbers.

A — Allocate It

Before spending, assign every naira a purpose.

Money without purpose disappears.

S — Strengthen It

Can part of this money become an asset?

Can it buy knowledge?

Can it increase future income?

Can it generate passive income?

H — Honour It

Treat money with respect.

Avoid careless spending.

Honour money by making wise decisions with it.

Money responds well to discipline.

Framework #1: The Wealth Bucket Model

Imagine your income flowing into five buckets.

- Bucket One – Living Expenses
- Bucket Two – Emergency Fund
- Bucket Three – Investments

- Bucket Four – Growth (Books, Courses, Skills)
- Bucket Five – Giving

Every bucket serves a purpose. When one bucket consumes everything, your financial life becomes unbalanced.

The Danger of Emotional Spending

Have you ever bought something simply because you were:

- Happy?
- Sad?
- Bored?
- Angry?
- Trying to impress someone?

Emotional spending is one of the silent destroyers of wealth. Retail therapy often creates financial regret.

Instead of asking,

"Can I afford this?"

Ask,

"Does this purchase move me closer to the life I want?"

The 24-Hour Rule

One simple habit can save you thousands.

For any non-essential purchase above your predetermined limit, wait 24 hours.

The excitement fades.

Logic returns.

Many unnecessary purchases disappear.

Financial maturity often looks like patience.

Framework #2: The Spending Decision Matrix

Before making any non-essential purchase, score it against each of these five questions using the scale below:

Scoring Guide

1 = Very Low / Not at all

2 = Low

3 = Moderate

4 = High

5 = Very High

How to Interpret Your Score

- **21–25 points:** Buy with confidence. This purchase aligns well with your financial priorities.
- **16–20 points:** A reasonable purchase. Proceed if it fits comfortably within your budget.
- **11–15 points:** Pause before buying. Wait 24 hours and reassess whether you still need it.

- **5–10 points:** Don't buy it. You're likely making an emotional purchase rather than a wise financial decision.

Remember:

Wise spending isn't about asking, "*Can I afford it?*" It's about asking, "*Is this the best use of my money?*"

The Power of Tracking

What gets measured gets managed.

Most people know:

- Their phone password
- Their favourite sports team
- Their social media analytics

Yet they cannot tell you how much they spent last month on food, transport, entertainment, or online shopping.

Tracking expenses is not punishment; it is awareness, and awareness creates improvement.

Case Study

Ada earns ₦800,000 every month but never budgets. She spends as needs arise and, at the end of every month, she wonders where her money went.

David also earns ₦800,000. Before the month begins, every naira already has a job:

- Living expenses
- Savings

- Investments
- Insurance
- Learning
- Giving

At the end of the year, both earned the same income.

One accumulated stress.

The other accumulated assets.

Money did not treat them differently; their systems did.

The Biggest Money Leaks

Watch out for these silent wealth destroyers:

- Lifestyle inflation
- Unplanned subscriptions
- Impulse purchases
- Consumer debt
- Keeping up with social media lifestyles
- Ignoring small daily expenses

Small leaks sink big ships.

Wealth Worksheet

My Monthly Money Map

Monthly Income: ₦____________________

Essential Expenses: ₦____________________

Savings: ₦__________________

Investments: ₦__________________

Learning: ₦__________________

Giving: ₦__________________

Entertainment: ₦__________________

Money Wasted Last Month: ₦__________________

What surprised me most? __________________

Wealth Checkpoint

Can you answer these questions?

- ☐ Do I know exactly how much I spend?
- ☐ Am I paying myself first?
- ☐ Am I investing consistently?
- ☐ Where is my biggest money leak?

If you cannot answer these questions confidently, your money is managing you more than you are managing it.

Wealth Challenge

For the next 30 days:

- ✓ Track every naira you spend.
- ✓ Eliminate one unnecessary expense.
- ✓ Increase your savings rate by at least 5%.

- ✓ Invest before you spend.
- ✓ Conduct a weekly Money Review check every Sunday evening.

Remember:

Financial freedom is not built through occasional big decisions.

It is built through thousands of small, intentional money decisions made consistently over time.

Because every naira you direct today is helping to design the wealth you will enjoy tomorrow.

Chapter Five

The Wealth-Building Formula

Wealth Marble

Wealth is not built by what you earn occasionally. It is built by what you consistently keep, grow, and multiply.

One of the biggest financial myths I have encountered is the belief that wealth belongs only to high-income earners.

Nothing could be further from the truth.

I have seen people with modest incomes quietly build substantial wealth through discipline, consistency, and wise decisions.

I have also seen people earning extraordinary incomes remain trapped in financial anxiety because they never developed the habits required to preserve and multiply what they earned.

The journey to wealth is not reserved for a privileged few.

It is available to anyone willing to embrace the right principles and remain committed to the process.

Every skyscraper begins with a single block.

Every mighty tree begins with a seed.

Every great fortune begins with one intentional financial decision.

Many people spend their lives searching for a secret formula to wealth.

They attend seminars.

Watch countless videos.

Follow successful entrepreneurs.

Study investment trends.

Yet they often overlook one simple truth:

Wealth is not a mystery; it is a process.

It is not built in one extraordinary moment.

It is built through ordinary decisions repeated consistently over time.

People who build lasting wealth understand that there is no shortcut around discipline.

The real formula has never changed.

Earn wisely.

Spend intentionally.

Save consistently.

Invest strategically.

Multiply patiently.

Repeat.

What Is the Wealth-Building Formula?

The Wealth-Building Formula is a simple but powerful process that transforms earned income into lasting financial independence.

Income alone does not create wealth.

Many people earn impressive salaries but remain financially vulnerable because every naira they earn immediately flows back out through lifestyle expenses.

The objective is not simply to earn money; the objective is to convert income into assets that continue producing value long after today's work is finished.

The Wealth Mentor Blueprint™

The G.R.O.W. Formula

Every wealth builder follows four essential stages.

G – Generate Income

Every wealth journey begins with earning.

Increase your value.

Develop marketable skills.

Build your expertise.

Solve meaningful problems.

The marketplace rewards those who create value.

The greater the value you create, the greater your earning potential.

R – Retain More Than You Spend

This is where many financial journeys fail.

It doesn't matter how much you earn if you spend everything.

Pay yourself first.

Live below your means.

Resist lifestyle inflation.

Saving is not a punishment, it is paying your future self.

O – Own Appreciating Assets

Money sitting idle loses value over time.

Money invested wisely creates more money.

Assets may include:

- Stocks
- Mutual Funds
- Real Estate
- Businesses
- Bonds
- Intellectual Property
- Digital Assets

The wealthy focus on ownership.

Not just consumption.

W – Watch Your Money Multiply

Time is one of the greatest wealth-building tools ever created.

The magic of compounding rewards patience.

Every investment today becomes tomorrow's opportunity.

Consistency beats intensity.

Small, regular investments often outperform occasional large ones because they build momentum over time.

FRAMEWORK #1

The Wealth Multiplication Cycle

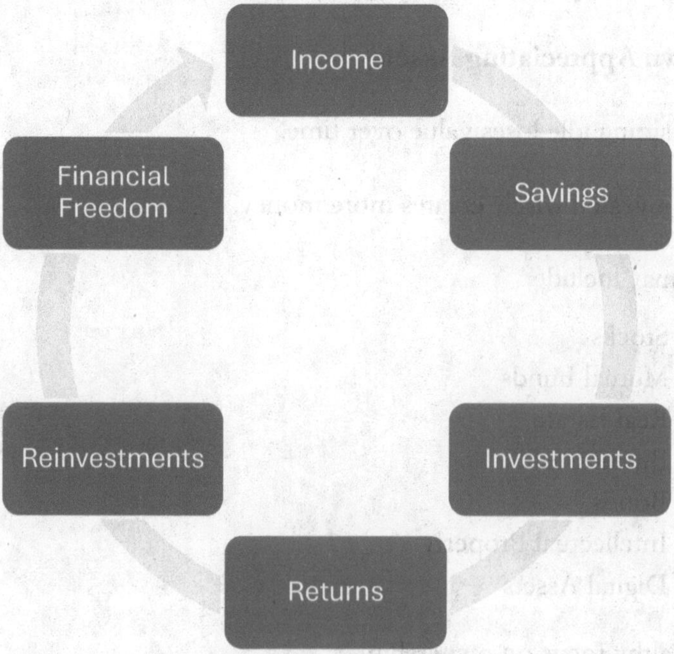

Notice that income appears only once.

Every other stage is about making your money work harder than you do.

The goal is to move from earning money to creating systems where money continues producing income on your behalf.

The Power of Compounding

Albert Einstein is often credited with calling compound interest one of the most powerful forces in finance. Whether or not he said those exact words, the principle remains true.

Compounding allows today's disciplined decisions to become tomorrow's financial breakthroughs.

A young professional who invests consistently over thirty years can accumulate significantly more wealth than someone who starts later, even if the later investor contributes larger amounts.

Time is an investor's greatest advantage.

Never underestimate the value of starting early.

The Enemy of Wealth

There are five silent enemies that quietly destroy wealth before it has the opportunity to grow.

- Lifestyle inflation
- Procrastination
- Consumer debt
- Lack of financial education
- Inconsistency

None of these happens overnight. They grow gradually.

That is why wealth builders develop systems rather than relying on motivation.

Framework #2: The 1-3-5 Wealth Accelerator

Every year, challenge yourself to:

- Build at least one new source of income.
- Increase your savings and investment rate by at least 3%.
- Acquire five new financial or business skills through books, courses, mentors, or practical experience.

This simple framework ensures that each year you earn more, know more, and own more. Small improvements, compounded over many years, yield extraordinary results.

Case Study

Two colleagues, Daniel and Tolu, each earn ₦700,000 per month.

Daniel spends first and saves whatever is left at the end of the month. Most months, nothing is left.

Tolu follows a different approach. The moment his salary arrives, he automatically transfers a percentage of it into savings and investments before spending anything else.

Five years later, Daniel has memories of many enjoyable purchases but little to show for them financially.

Tolu has built an emergency fund, an investment portfolio, and ownership in two additional income-generating ventures.

Both earned the same salary.

The difference was never income.

The difference was the system they followed.

Wealth Worksheet

My Wealth-Building Formula

Current monthly income: ₦ ____________________

Current savings rate: ________ %

Current investment rate: ________ %

Assets I currently own: ____________________

Assets I want to own in the next five years: __________

One income stream I will build this year: __________

Wealth Checkpoint

Ask yourself honestly:

- ☐ Am I living below my means?
- ☐ Am I consistently investing?
- ☐ Is my money working for me?
- ☐ What percentage of my income becomes an asset each month?
- ☐ Am I building wealth or simply financing my lifestyle?

Wealth Challenge

For the next 90 days:

- ✓ Increase your savings rate by at least 3%.
- ✓ Start or increase an automatic investment plan.
- ✓ Read one book on investing or wealth creation.
- ✓ Identify one new income opportunity.
- ✓ Track your net worth at the beginning and end of the challenge.

Remember:

Building wealth is not about one brilliant financial decision.

It is about hundreds of wise decisions repeated consistently.

Every asset you acquire, every investment you make, and every disciplined financial habit you develop brings you one step closer to financial freedom.

Wealth is never an accident.

It is intentionally designed, patiently built, and faithfully multiplied.

Chapter Six

Investing For Growth and Security

Wealth Marble

Money that sleeps in your account grows older. Money that is wisely invested grows stronger.

Many people spend decades working for money but never reach financial freedom because they never learn to make money work for them. This chapter will help you understand how to think like an investor, avoid costly mistakes, and position your money for long-term growth.

Wealth Mentor's Note

One of the biggest mistakes people make is believing that saving and investing are the same thing. They are not.

Saving protects money. Investing grows money. Both are necessary.

Savings give you security. Investments give you freedom.

The goal is not simply to accumulate money.

The goal is to position your money where it has the opportunity to multiply over time.

That is the difference between financial survival and financial independence.

Imagine planting a seed.

Instead of placing it in fertile soil, you keep it safely inside your drawer.

Years later, the seed is still there.

Safe. Untouched. But completely unproductive.

Many people treat their money exactly the same way.

They work hard. Earn an income. Save faithfully. Then leave their money sitting idle for years.

While they have protected it, they have not positioned it to grow.

Inflation quietly reduces its purchasing power.

Opportunities pass by. Time continues moving.

Money, like a seed, must be planted wisely if it is to multiply.

Investing is simply giving your money the opportunity to grow beyond what your labour alone can produce.

Why Investing Matters

There are only two ways to increase your income:

- You can continue working harder for money.
- Or you can allow your money to begin working for you.

The first approach has limits.

There are only twenty-four hours in a day.

The second approach has far greater potential.

Proper investing allows your income to continue growing even while you sleep, travel, or spend time with your family.

That is why investing is not optional for anyone who desires long-term financial freedom.

The Difference Between Saving and Investing

Saving is storing money for future use.

Investing is putting money to work for future growth.

Savings provide stability.

Investments create prosperity.

Think of savings as your safety net.

Think of investments as your ladder.

Both are essential, but one protects your future while the other builds it.

The Wealth Mentor Blueprint™

The P.L.A.N.T. Framework

Every successful investment follows five principles.

P — Prepare

Never invest money you cannot afford to leave untouched for a period of time.

Build your emergency fund first.

Pay off high-interest debt.

Invest from a position of strength—not desperation.

L — Learn

Never invest in what you do not understand.

If you cannot explain how an investment works, you should not invest in it.

Knowledge is your first investment.

The more you understand, the better your decisions become.

A — Assess

Every investment carries some level of risk. Ask:

- What is the expected return?
- What are the risks?
- How long is my money likely to be tied up?
- Who regulates this investment?
- What is the worst-case scenario?

Never allow excitement to replace due diligence.

N — Nurture

Investing is not gambling.

It requires patience.

Do not uproot your investment every time the market fluctuates.

Healthy investments need time to mature.

T — Think Long Term

The greatest returns often belong to those who remain disciplined over many years.

Short-term emotions destroy long-term wealth.

Invest with decades in mind, not days.

Framework #1: The Investment Pyramid

Level One: Emergency Fund

Level Two: Insurance and Protection

Level Three: Retirement Investments

Level Four: Growth Investments

- Stocks
- Mutual Funds
- Real Estate
- Businesses

Level Five: Alternative Investments

- Private Equity
- Intellectual Property
- Digital Businesses
- Global Opportunities

Build your investments from the bottom upward.

Strong foundations produce lasting wealth.

The Golden Rules of Investing

Rule One: Never invest because of pressure.

Rule Two: Never invest because everyone else is investing.

Rule Three: Never invest money meant for school fees, rent, or emergency needs.

Rule Four: Never chase unrealistic returns. If it sounds too good to be true, it probably is.

Rule Five: Invest consistently. Small, regular investments often outperform large, occasional investments.

The Power of Compounding

Compounding is wealth's best friend.

Imagine planting one fruit tree. Years later, it produces many fruits.

Inside every fruit are more seeds. Those seeds become more trees. Those trees produce more fruit.

That is compounding.

Money earns returns. Those returns begin earning returns.

Eventually, your returns begin producing returns of their own.

Time transforms ordinary investing into extraordinary wealth.

This is why your greatest investment advantage is not necessarily how much money you have.

It is how early you begin.

Framework #2: The 5-5-5 Investment Filter

Before committing money to any investment, ask yourself five questions:

- Do I understand it?
- Do I trust the people behind it?
- Can I comfortably leave my money invested for at least five years?
- Does it align with my financial goals?
- If I lost this investment, would my financial life collapse?

If you answer "No" to several of these questions, pause.

The best investment opportunities are not the fastest.

They are the wisest.

The Biggest Investment Mistakes

Avoid these costly traps:

- Investing based on rumours.
- Following social media hype.
- Trying to get rich overnight.
- Putting all your money into one investment.

- Ignoring risk.
- Failing to diversify.
- Waiting forever for the "perfect" time.

The greatest investment risk is often doing nothing at all.

Case Study

Chioma and Michael each receive a ₦5 million bonus.

Michael buys a luxury SUV. Five years later, the car has depreciated significantly.

Chioma uses part of her bonus to build an emergency fund and invests the balance across diversified assets aligned with her goals. Over time, those investments appreciate and begin generating additional income.

Both enjoyed the reward of their hard work.

One bought a depreciating lifestyle.

The other built appreciating wealth.

The difference was not the money they received.

The difference was the decision they made.

Wealth Worksheet

My Investment Readiness Assessment

Emergency Fund: □ Yes □ No

Outstanding High-Interest Debt: ₦__________________

Monthly Amount Available for Investing: ₦__________________

Current Investments: ₦ ____________________

Investment Knowledge Level: Beginner □ Intermediate □ Advanced □

Three Investment Areas I Want to Learn About:

(i)_______________ (ii)_____________ (iii) ________________

My Long-Term Investment Goal: ___________________

Wealth Checkpoint

- ☐ Do I understand every investment I currently own?
- ☐ Am I investing consistently?
- ☐ Is my portfolio diversified?
- ☐ Am I investing for the long term?
- ☐ Is my money working as hard as I do?

Wealth Challenge

Over the next 30 days:

- ✓ Read one book about investing.
- ✓ Learn about one investment vehicle you have never explored before.
- ✓ Review your current portfolio.
- ✓ Identify one unnecessary expense you can redirect towards investing.

✓ Create an automatic monthly investment plan.

Remember:

Investing is not about predicting the future; it is about preparing for it.

Every wise investment you make today is a seed planted for tomorrow's harvest.

Money grows where wisdom leads.

The future belongs not only to those who earn well, but to those who invest wisely.

Part Three

EXPANDING YOUR WEALTH

Chapter Seven
The Power of Multiple Income Streams

> *Wealth Marble*
>
> *One income stream may pay your bills, but multiple income streams build your freedom.*

Imagine trying to sit comfortably on a one-legged chair. No matter how strong that single leg is, it takes only one unexpected shift for everything to collapse.

That is exactly what happens when your entire financial life depends on one source of income.

A job loss.
A business slowdown.
An economic recession.
A health challenge.
A global crisis.

Any one of these can suddenly interrupt your income and disrupt your lifestyle.

The lesson is simple: financial security is not determined by how much you earn from one source; it is determined by how many reliable sources of income you have.

This chapter will help you understand how to build additional income streams strategically without abandoning your current responsibilities.

Wealth Mentor's Note

One of the greatest financial mistakes I see is people waiting until they are in financial trouble before looking for another source of income.

By then, desperation often replaces good judgment.

The best time to build another income stream is while your primary income is still stable.

You do not build an umbrella when the rain has already started; you prepare before the storm. That is how financially wise people think.

Every successful business understands the danger of relying on only one customer. If that customer leaves, the business may collapse.

Yet many people build their entire financial lives around one employer, one client, or one source of income. They hope it will always be enough.

Hope is not a financial strategy.

The world has changed.

Technology has changed.

Work has changed.

Opportunities have changed.

Today, wealth is no longer built only by working harder, it is built by creating multiple pathways through which value flows back to you.

That is the power of multiple income streams.

What Is An Income Stream?

An income stream is any source that consistently generates money for you. It may come from:

- Your skills.
- Your investments.
- Your business.
- Your intellectual property.

Or your assets.

The goal is not to have many jobs; the goal is to build multiple sources of value that generate income over time.

The Difference Between Active and Passive Income

Active Income

Money earned through your direct effort. Examples include:

- Salary
- Professional services
- Consulting
- Freelancing

If you stop working, the income usually stops.

Passive Income

Money earned with limited ongoing effort after the initial work has been done. Examples include:

- Dividends
- Rental income
- Royalties
- Digital products
- Online courses
- Investments

Passive income does not mean "no work." It means you do the work once and continue benefiting from it over time.

The Wealth Mentor Blueprint™

The B.U.I.L.D. Framework

Every sustainable income stream follows five stages.

B – Build Valuable Skills

Your greatest asset is not your money; it is your ability to solve problems.

Skills create opportunities.

The more valuable your skills become, the greater your earning potential.

U – Understand Market Needs

People pay for solutions.

Find problems worth solving.

The marketplace rewards relevance.

Don't ask,

"What do I want to sell?"

Ask,

"What problem can I solve?"

I – Increase Your Value

Read.
Learn.
Network.

Improve your communication.

Develop leadership.

Invest in yourself before expecting others to invest in you.

L – Launch Small

Do not wait for perfection.

Test your ideas by starting with:
One client.
One product.
One service.
One investment.

Small beginnings often lead to extraordinary outcomes.

D – Diversify Wisely

Build additional income streams gradually.

Do not chase every opportunity.

Focus on quality rather than quantity.

Each new stream should strengthen your financial foundation rather than distract you from it.

Framework #1: The Income Ladder

Level 1: Salary or Wages

Level 2: Freelancing or Consulting

Level 3: Business Income

Level 4: Investment Income

Level 5: Passive Income

Level 6: Legacy Income

The objective is not to skip levels. It is to climb them intentionally.

Where Can Additional Income Come From?

Consider opportunities such as:

- Professional consulting
- Digital products
- Public speaking
- Writing books
- Coaching

- Agriculture
- Real estate
- Dividend-paying investments
- Online businesses
- Licensing intellectual property
- Content creation
- Affiliate marketing

The possibilities continue to expand in today's digital economy. The key is choosing opportunities that align with your skills, interests, and long-term goals.

The Biggest Mistakes People Make

- Chasing every trending opportunity.
- Starting too many ventures at once.
- Ignoring their primary source of income.
- Expecting instant success.
- Failing to develop the necessary skills.
- Confusing busyness with productivity.

Remember:

More income streams should increase your freedom—not your confusion.

Framework #2: The 3–2–1 Wealth Expansion Plan

Every year aim to:

- Develop 3 new high-income skills.
- Create 2 additional sources of income.
- Acquire 1 income-producing asset.

This simple strategy, repeated consistently over several years, can transform your financial future. Small annual improvements create extraordinary long-term results.

Case Study

Amaka works as an accountant.

Instead of depending solely on her salary, she gradually develops additional income streams.

She starts offering bookkeeping services to small businesses on weekends. Later, she creates an online financial literacy course. She also invests consistently in dividend-paying assets.

Within five years, her salary is no longer her only source of income.

When her company restructures, she remains financially stable because she has built multiple pillars of support.

Her freedom did not come from working more hours; it came from building more pathways for income.

Wealth Worksheet

My Income Stream Planner

Current Primary Income: ____________________

Current Additional Income Streams: ____________________

Skills I Can Monetise: ____________________

One New Income Stream I Can Start Within 90 Days: ______

Income Goal for the Next Three Years: ____________________

Wealth Checkpoint

☐ Am I relying on only one source of income?

☐ What valuable skill can I monetise?

☐ Which of my current skills is underutilised?

☐ Am I building assets that generate income?

☐ If my primary income stopped today, how long could I sustain my lifestyle?

Wealth Challenge

Over the next 90 days:

✓ Learn one new marketable skill.

✓ Research three additional income opportunities.

✓ Start one small income-generating project.

✓ Invest in one income-producing asset.

✓ Create a written plan for your second income stream.

Remember:

Multiple income streams are not about becoming busy, they are about becoming resilient.

Financial freedom is rarely built on one source of income.

It is built through multiple streams of value flowing into your life.

Because when your income grows from many roots, your financial future becomes much stronger.

Chapter Eight

Creating Value Before Seeking Profit

Wealth Marble

The marketplace does not reward your needs. It rewards the value you create.

Many people spend years asking one question:

"How can I make more money?"

It seems like the right question. But it isn't.

A better question is:

"How can I become more valuable?"

Money is attracted to value.

Promotion follows value.

Business growth follows value.

Influence follows value.

The wealthiest people in the world did not become wealthy because they chased money.

They became wealthy because they solved problems that millions of people were willing to pay for.

If you spend your life chasing money, you may never have enough.

But if you spend your life creating value, money will spend its life chasing you.

This chapter will completely change the way you think about wealth.

Wealth Mentor's Note

One lesson I have learned over the years is this:

Value is the product, while money is a by-product.

Whenever I focus on adding value, opportunities follow, relationships grow, businesses expand, and income increases.

The temptation is always to ask,

"What can I get?"

Successful people ask a different question:

"What can I give?"

The moment you become valuable enough, the marketplace cannot ignore you.

Imagine two restaurants opening on the same street.

The first focuses only on making money.

The second focuses on serving delicious meals, creating memorable experiences, maintaining excellent hygiene, and delighting every customer.

Which one do you think will still be thriving five years later?

Customers rarely return because a business wants profit; they return because they receive value.

The same principle applies to every profession.

People do not pay you because you need money, they pay you because you solve problems.

Profit is simply the reward for consistently creating value.

What Is Value?

Value is anything that improves another person's life, solves a problem, saves time, reduces stress, creates opportunities, or produces meaningful results.

Value is not limited to products.

A teacher creates value by educating.

A doctor creates value by restoring health.

An engineer creates value by solving technical challenges.

A farmer creates value by feeding communities.

A writer creates value through ideas.

A banker creates value by helping individuals and businesses manage and grow their finances.

Every profession creates wealth by first creating value.

Why Value Always Wins

Money follows value because value creates trust.

Trust creates relationships.

Relationships create opportunities.

Opportunities create income.

Income creates wealth.

Many people try to skip this process. They pursue income before value. Eventually, the marketplace exposes the difference.

Long-term success belongs to those who consistently improve the lives of others.

The Wealth Mentor Blueprint™

The V.A.L.U.E. Framework

Every financially successful person intentionally develops these five habits.

V — Visualise Problems

Successful people see problems differently.

Where others complain, they see opportunities.

Every problem waiting to be solved is a potential business waiting to be built.

A — Add Meaningful Solutions

Do not compete only on price, compete on value.

Ask yourself daily:

- How can I make someone's life easier?
- How can I improve this experience?
- How can I serve better?

L — Learn Continuously

Your income rarely outgrows your knowledge for long.

The more valuable your knowledge becomes, the more valuable your contribution becomes.

Invest in yourself first, everything else follows.

U — Understand People

Value is determined by the receiver, not the giver.

Learn what people genuinely need.

Listen carefully.

Observe constantly.

Serve intentionally.

E — Expand Your Influence

Never stop improving.

Never stop innovating.

Never stop serving.

The greater your influence, the greater your opportunities to create value.

Framework #1: The Value Ladder

Level 1: Solve Your Own Problems

Level 2: Solve Problems for Individuals

Level 3: Solve Problems for Businesses

Level 4: Solve Problems for Communities

Level 5: Solve Problems at Scale

The more people you help, the greater the value you create.

The greater the value you create, the greater the wealth you can build.

The Law of Exchange

Every financial transaction is simply an exchange of value.

People exchange money for something they consider more valuable.

- Knowledge
- Convenience.
- Security
- Entertainment
- Health
- Speed

- Results

If people are unwilling to pay for what you offer, ask yourself:

"How can I increase the value?"

Not,

"How can I increase the price?"

Framework #2: The Value Multiplier

Before launching any product, service, or business idea, ask yourself these five questions:

- What problem am I solving?
- Who has this problem?
- Why does this problem matter?
- How is my solution different or better?
- How can I create even more value than people expect?

When you consistently exceed expectations, people remember you.

They recommend you.

They return to you.

Value creates loyalty.

The Greatest Investment

The highest-return investment you will ever make is not necessarily in stocks, real estate, or businesses. It is in yourself.

Every new skill.
Every book.
Every mentor.
Every course.
Every experience.
Every lesson.

They all increase your capacity to create value. And as your value grows, so does your earning potential.

Case Study

Grace and Daniel both start consulting businesses.

Grace spends most of her energy trying to attract clients.

Daniel spends his time becoming exceptional at solving clients' problems.

He studies. He improves. He delivers beyond expectations.

Within three years, Grace is still chasing customers, while Daniel is turning customers away because of referrals.

The difference was not marketing.

The difference was value.

Wealth Worksheet

My Personal Value Audit

- What problem do I solve? ______________________
- Who benefits most from my skills? ____________________
- What skill can I improve this year? ____________________
- How can I create more value in my current job or business? ________________________
- What unique strength distinguishes me from others? _____

Wealth Checkpoint

☐ What value do I consistently create?

☐ What problem am I known for solving?

☐ How am I investing in my knowledge?

☐ Am I chasing money or creating value?

☐ If my income doubled tomorrow, would my value justify it?

Wealth Challenge

Over the next 30 days:

✓ Read one book that strengthens your expertise.

✓ Learn one new skill that increases your value.

✓ Solve one problem without expecting immediate reward.

✓ Ask five people how you can improve the value you provide.

- ✓ Write a personal Value Statement describing the impact you want to create.

Remember:

Money is a reward. Value is the reason.

If you commit yourself to becoming more valuable every day, wealth will no longer be something you chase. It will become something you attract.

Because the marketplace will always reward people who make other people's lives better.

Never Forget: Profit is the applause. Value is the performance.

Chapter Nine

Entrepreneurship and Economic Empowerment

Wealth Marble

Entrepreneurs don't wait for opportunities. They develop the eyes to see problems, the courage to solve them, and the discipline to build value around them.

Many people believe entrepreneurship is simply about starting a business. It isn't.
Entrepreneurship is a way of thinking.

It is the ability to identify opportunities where others see obstacles.

It is the courage to create solutions instead of excuses.

It is the discipline to build something valuable long before anyone recognises its worth.

In today's rapidly changing world, entrepreneurial thinking is no longer optional.

Whether you work in a multinational organisation, own a small business, lead a ministry, or are still in school, the ability to think entrepreneurially will determine how much value you create and how much impact you make.

This chapter will help you cultivate the mindset, habits, and practical strategies needed to become an opportunity creator rather than an opportunity seeker.

Wealth Mentor's Note

One of the greatest misconceptions about entrepreneurship is that it begins with capital.

It doesn't.

It begins with curiosity.

Capital can build a business; but only vision can create one.

Every successful entrepreneur first noticed something others ignored.

A problem.
A gap.
An inefficiency.
A need.

Money simply helped them scale the solution.

Never allow a lack of capital to become an excuse for a lack of creativity.

Your first investment is not money; it is your ability to observe, think, and solve.

Imagine walking through a crowded market.

Thousands of people pass through every day.

Some see only buyers and sellers: others see opportunities.

One person notices that shoppers struggle to carry multiple bags.

Another notices that vendors need better payment solutions.

Someone else realises there is demand for home delivery.

The market is the same. The difference is perspective.

Entrepreneurs see possibilities hidden inside everyday problems.

That is why entrepreneurship is less about business registration and more about opportunity recognition.

What Is Entrepreneurship?

Entrepreneurship is the intentional process of identifying problems, creating solutions, and building sustainable systems that generate value, income, and impact.

Notice the order:

Problems.
Solutions.
Value.
Income.
Impact.

Money is never the starting point. Value is.

The Entrepreneurial Mindset

Entrepreneurs ask different questions.

Instead of asking,

"Where can I find a job?"

They ask,

"What problem can I solve?"

Instead of asking,

"Who will employ me?"

They ask,

"How can I create opportunities for myself and others?"

This shift in thinking changes everything.

The Wealth Mentor Blueprint™

The C.R.E.A.T.E. Framework™

Every successful entrepreneur consistently practices these six principles.

C – Curiosity

Stay curious.

Observe your environment.

Ask questions.

The next business opportunity may be hiding inside an everyday inconvenience.

R – Research

Before launching an idea, understand the market.

Who needs your solution?

How are they solving it today?

How can you serve them better?

Never build a business on assumptions.

Build it on understanding.

E – Execute

Ideas have no value until they are implemented.

Many brilliant ideas remain trapped inside notebooks.

Progress belongs to those who take action.

Start before everything is perfect.

A – Adapt

Markets change.

Technology changes.

Customer expectations change.

Entrepreneurs who refuse to adapt eventually become irrelevant.

Flexibility is a competitive advantage.

T – Trust

Build trust before expecting loyalty.

People buy from businesses they believe in.

Trust is earned through consistency, honesty, quality, and excellent service.

E – Expand

Once your solution works consistently, improve it.

Systemise it.

Scale it.

Create new opportunities from existing success.

Growth should be intentional—not accidental.

Framework #1: The Opportunity Circle™

Every successful business begins with this simple cycle:

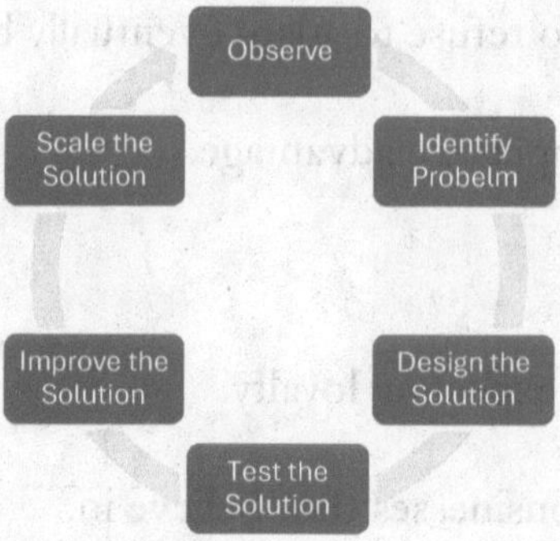

Do not fall in love with your idea.

Fall in love with solving the problem.

The Four Types of Entrepreneurs

The Opportunity Entrepreneur: Sees possibilities before others.

The Innovation Entrepreneur: Creates new ways of solving existing problems.

The Service Entrepreneur: Builds wealth by consistently serving people well.

The Impact Entrepreneur: Measures success not only by profit, but by the lives transformed.

The greatest entrepreneurs often combine all four.

Framework #2: The 5P Business Test™

Before starting any business, ask yourself these five questions:

1. Problem: What specific problem am I solving?

2. People: Who has this problem?

3. Product: What solution am I offering?

4. Profitability: Can this solution generate sustainable income?

5. Purpose: Beyond making money, what impact will this business create?

If your business passes all five tests, you have a stronger foundation for long-term success.

The Biggest Entrepreneurial Mistakes

Avoid these common traps:

- Starting because everyone else is doing it
- Ignoring customer feedback
- Trying to grow too quickly
- Failing to understand cash flow
- Refusing to adapt
- Chasing profit while neglecting value

Businesses grow when customers win.

Case Study

Aisha works full-time in a bank. She notices that many small business owners struggle with bookkeeping and financial planning.

Instead of resigning from her job immediately, she begins offering financial advisory services on weekends. She listens carefully to her clients, improves her services, and builds a reputation for excellence.

As demand grows, she creates templates, online resources, and digital courses.

Years later, her business generates multiple streams of income while continuing to create meaningful value.

She did not begin with millions; she began by solving one problem well.

Wealth Worksheet

My Entrepreneurial Blueprint

- What problem frustrates me the most? ________________
- Who experiences this problem? ________________
- How could I solve it differently? ________________
- What skills do I already have? ________________
- What skills do I still need? ________________
- What small step can I take within the next 30 days? ______

Wealth Checkpoint

☐ Have I identified a genuine problem worth solving?

☐ Do I understand my target audience?

☐ Am I creating value before expecting profit?

☐ What unique advantage do I bring?

☐ Am I willing to start small and grow steadily?

Wealth Challenge

Over the next 30 days:

✓ Identify five problems you encounter in everyday life.

✓ Choose one problem that genuinely interests you.

✓ Speak with at least ten people who experience that problem.

✓ Develop one simple solution.

✓ Take one practical step towards turning that solution into a business or income-generating opportunity.

Remember:

Entrepreneurship is not reserved for a select few.

It is available to anyone willing to think differently, solve problems consistently, and create value with excellence.

Because every thriving business was once nothing more than an idea supported by courage, discipline, and action.

And Never Forget: Opportunities are rarely found. They are created.

Part Four

PROTECTING AND MULTIPLYING WEALTH

Chapter Ten

Financial Wisdom for Sustainable Impact

Wealth Marble

Money is a wonderful servant, but a terrible master. The greatest measure of wealth is not how much you accumulate, but how wisely you steward what has been entrusted to you.

Many people know how to make money. Far fewer know how to keep it. Even fewer know how to use it wisely. History is filled with people who accumulated enormous wealth yet left behind financial confusion, broken families, failed businesses, and wasted opportunities.

Why?

Because making money and managing wealth requires two different kinds of intelligence.

Money can be earned through talent. But wealth is sustained through wisdom.

Financial wisdom is what transforms temporary success into lasting significance.

This chapter is about becoming not just a wealth creator, but a faithful steward.

Because wealth that lacks wisdom rarely survives.

Wealth Mentor's Note

There is a question I have learned to ask myself before every significant financial decision.

Not...

"Can I afford it?"

Not even...

"Will it make me money?"

But...

"Will this decision strengthen the future I am intentionally designing?"

That single question has changed the way I think about money.

Every financial decision is shaping someone.

Either your present self, or your future self.

Wisdom teaches us to honour the future.

Imagine giving a teenager the keys to a high-performance sports car without teaching them how to drive.

The car is not the problem, the lack of wisdom is.

Money works the same way.

Money amplifies character, it magnifies habits, and it exposes priorities.

Placed in wise hands, money creates opportunities.

Placed in careless hands, the same money creates problems.

That is why the pursuit of wisdom must always be greater than the pursuit of wealth.

What Is Financial Wisdom?

Financial wisdom is the ability to make decisions today that continue producing value tomorrow.

It is not about how much money you have, but how wisely you use what you have.

Financial wisdom teaches us that every naira has a purpose.

Every investment has a consequence.

Every financial decision leaves a footprint.

Wise people think beyond today's transaction. They think about tomorrow's impact.

The Difference Between Knowledge and Wisdom

Knowledge tells you how to invest. Wisdom tells you when to invest.

Knowledge tells you how to make money. Wisdom tells you how to keep your integrity while making it.

Knowledge shows you opportunity. Wisdom helps you recognise timing.

Knowledge fills your mind. Wisdom guides your decisions.

That is why wisdom is wealth's greatest companion.

The Wealth Mentor Blueprint™

The S.T.E.W.A.R.D. Framework™

Every financially wise person develops these seven habits:

S — Spend Intentionally

Every purchase should reflect your priorities.

Never allow emotions to become your financial adviser.

T — Think Long-Term

Temporary pleasure should never destroy permanent opportunities.

Every financial decision should honour your future.

E — Eliminate Waste

Waste is not always expensive.

Sometimes it arrives disguised as "small daily habits."

Small leaks eventually sink great ships.

W — Work With Purpose

Money earned without purpose often disappears without purpose.

Know why you work.

Know why you earn.

Know why you build wealth.

A — Appreciate What You Have

Gratitude protects us from endless comparison.

Contentment is not the enemy of ambition.

It is the guardian of peace.

R — Reinvest Continuously

Never consume everything you produce.

Every harvest should provide seed for the next season.

D — Design Your Legacy

Every financial decision should move you closer to the life—and legacy—you want to leave behind.

FRAMEWORK #1: The Wealth Stewardship Circle™

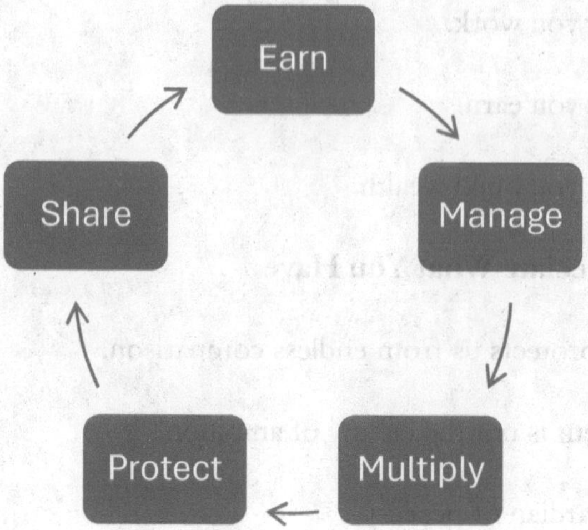

Notice something interesting; the cycle never ends.

Wealth is not a destination. It is a lifelong stewardship journey.

The Three Questions of Financial Wisdom

Before every major financial decision, ask yourself:

- Will this strengthen me?
- Will this strengthen my family?
- Will this strengthen my future?

If the answer is "No" to all three... pause.

Wisdom often speaks through patience.

Framework #2: The 10-10-10 Impact Filter™

Before making any major financial decision, ask yourself:

10 Days: How will I feel about this decision in ten days?

10 Months: Will this decision still benefit me ten months from now?

10 Years: Will this decision move me closer to the legacy I hope to build?

The longer your thinking...The wiser your decisions.

The Hidden Cost of Impulse

Every purchase has two prices.

The first is what you pay today.

The second is the opportunity you lose tomorrow.

That expensive phone could have become an investment.

That unnecessary luxury could have become business capital.

That impulse purchase could have become financial freedom.

Wise people always calculate both prices.

Case Study

Emmanuel receives an unexpected bonus.

His friends encourage him to celebrate with expensive purchases.

Instead, he enjoys a modest celebration, clears outstanding debt, increases his investment portfolio, supports a meaningful cause, and reserves part of the money for future opportunities.

Five years later, the bonus has long been spent by everyone. But Emmanuel's wise decisions continue producing returns.

Money disappears.

Wisdom continues paying dividends.

Wealth Worksheet

My Stewardship Assessment

When I receive unexpected income, I usually _______________

The three biggest areas where I waste money are:

1. __________________

2. __________________

3. __________________

One financial habit I must stop immediately: ________________

One financial habit I must strengthen: ______________________

What kind of financial legacy am I building today? __________

Wealth Checkpoint

☐ Do my financial decisions reflect my values?

☐ Am I spending intentionally?

☐ Am I reinvesting consistently?

☐ Am I building wealth or merely enjoying income?

☐ Would my future self-thank me for today's decisions?

Wealth Challenge

For the next 30 days:

- ✓ Delay one unnecessary purchase every week.
- ✓ Redirect the money towards an investment.
- ✓ Review every expense above your personal spending limit.
- ✓ Perform one intentional act of generosity.
- ✓ Write your Personal Stewardship Statement.

Remember:

Money is not the destination; it is the vehicle.

Wisdom decides where that vehicle goes.

Because wealth without wisdom is temporary. But wealth guided by wisdom becomes a blessing that outlives its owner.

Never Forget: You are not merely managing money, you are managing possibilities. And the quality of your stewardship today determines the opportunities you will have tomorrow.

Chapter Eleven
Wealth Preservation Strategies

> *Wealth Marble*
>
> *Building wealth requires discipline. Preserving wealth requires wisdom. Losing wealth requires only neglect.*

Many people spend decades building wealth. Very few spend time learning how to preserve it. History is filled with fortunes that disappeared within a single generation.

Businesses that collapsed after their founders died.

Properties lost through poor planning.

Family wealth destroyed by conflict.

Investments wiped out through carelessness.

The tragedy is not that wealth was impossible to preserve; the tragedy is that preservation was never part of the plan.

Creating wealth is exciting. Protecting wealth requires maturity.

This chapter will help you understand how to safeguard what you have worked so hard to build.

Because wealth that is not protected rarely survives.

Wealth Mentor's Note

One lesson life has taught me is this:

People spend years learning how to make money, but very few spend time learning how to protect it.

Yet every successful builder understands something important; the stronger the building becomes, the stronger its protection must be.

The same principle applies to wealth.

The more you build, the more intentional you must become about protecting it, because every valuable thing attracts risk.

Imagine spending twenty years building your dream home. Every brick carefully laid. Every room thoughtfully designed. Every sacrifice worthwhile.

Then imagine leaving every door unlocked every night.

It wouldn't make sense.

Yet many people do exactly that with their finances. They build businesses without succession plans. Acquire assets without adequate protection. Invest without diversification. Create wealth without documentation.

Hope is not protection. Preparation is.

What Does It Mean to Preserve Wealth?

Wealth preservation is the intentional process of protecting your financial resources so they continue serving you, your family, and future generations.

Preservation is not fear; it is wisdom.

It recognises that every season of abundance should prepare for seasons of uncertainty.

Wise people do not prepare because they expect the worst.

They prepare because life is unpredictable.

What Threatens Wealth?

Wealth rarely disappears overnight. More often, it erodes gradually through poor decisions.

Some of the greatest threats include:

- Poor financial discipline
- Lifestyle inflation
- Unnecessary debt
- Lack of diversification
- Poor record keeping
- Fraud and scams
- Failure to plan for succession
- Ignoring legal and tax obligations
- Emotional financial decisions

Most fortunes are not destroyed by one major mistake.

They are weakened by many small ones.

The Wealth Mentor Blueprint™

The P.R.O.T.E.C.T. Framework™

Every lasting fortune is built on these seven principles.

P – Plan Ahead

Protection begins long before problems appear.

Think ahead.

Prepare ahead.

Document ahead.

R – Reduce Risk

Never place everything in one investment.

Diversify.

Protect yourself against avoidable losses.

Wisdom spreads risk.

O – Organise Your Financial Life

Keep proper records.

Know where your assets are.

Know your liabilities.

Know your obligations.

Clarity is protection.

T – Think Beyond Today

Every financial decision should consider tomorrow.

Protect your future before enjoying your present.

E – Establish Safeguards

Insurance.

Emergency funds.

Legal documentation.

Trusted professional advisers.

Protection is a system—not an event.

C – Continue Learning

The financial world changes constantly.

Remain informed.

Remain teachable.

Remain vigilant.

T – Transfer Wisely

Wealth that cannot be transferred is incomplete.

Prepare your family.

Prepare your business.

Prepare your legacy.

Framework #1

The Wealth Shield™

Every strong financial life should be protected by five shields.

Shield One: Emergency Fund

Shield Two: Insurance

Shield Three: Diversified Investments

Shield Four: Legal Documentation

Shield Five: Financial Knowledge

When one shield weakens, strengthen it before moving on.

Protection is layered.

The Cost of Ignoring Protection

Many people believe,

"It won't happen to me."

Until it does.

- A medical emergency
- A lawsuit

- A business downturn
- Identity theft
- Unexpected economic changes

Financial wisdom teaches us to prepare before pressure arrives.

Preparation transforms crisis into inconvenience.

Framework #2: The 5R Preservation Check™

Before making any major financial decision, ask:

- **Risk:** What could go wrong?
- **Return:** Is the reward worth the risk?
- **Resilience:** Can I recover if this fails?
- **Records:** Have I documented everything properly?
- **Responsibility:** Who else could be affected by this decision?

These five questions encourage careful thinking before taking significant financial risks.

The Role of Contentment

One of the greatest protectors of wealth is contentment.

Contentment does not mean a lack of ambition. It means freedom from unnecessary comparison.

Comparison often leads to overspending.

Overspending leads to debt.

Debt weakens wealth.

Peace often protects what pride destroys.

Case Study

Kunle builds a successful manufacturing business over twenty-five years. He invests wisely and acquires several valuable assets. However, he never documents ownership clearly, creates a succession plan, or prepares his family for leadership.

After his passing, disagreements arise. Legal disputes delay operations. Assets become difficult to access. Much of what he spent decades building begins to decline.

His challenge was never a lack of wealth.

It was a lack of preparation.

Now consider Amina. She builds steadily, keeps accurate records, reviews her investments regularly, consults trusted advisers, maintains appropriate insurance, and prepares her family to understand her financial vision.

When unexpected challenges arise, her financial foundation remains stable because she planned before the pressure came.

Both individuals worked hard.

Only one protected the future of what they built.

Wealth Worksheet

My Wealth Preservation Plan

Emergency Fund Status: □ Complete □ In Progress □ Not Started

- Do I have adequate insurance? ____________________
- Have I documented my major assets? ____________________
- Do I review my investments annually? ____________________

If something happened to me today, would my family know where my important financial records are? □ Yes □ No

One area of my financial life that needs stronger protection is: ____________________

Wealth Checkpoint

☐ Do I have an emergency fund?

☐ Am I adequately insured?

☐ Have I diversified my investments?

☐ Have I documented my financial affairs?

☐ Am I protecting my wealth as intentionally as I built it?

Wealth Challenge

Over the next 30 days:

✓ Create or strengthen your emergency fund.

- ✓ Review your insurance coverage.
- ✓ Organise all important financial documents.
- ✓ Update your list of assets and liabilities.
- ✓ Meet with a trusted financial or legal adviser to review your long-term protection strategy.

Remember:

It takes discipline to build wealth. It takes wisdom to preserve it.

The strongest financial legacy is not the one that grows the fastest; it is the one that endures the longest.

True wealth is measured not only by what you build, but by what you successfully protect for the generations that follow.

Part Five

FROM WEALTH TO LEGACY

Chapter Twelve

Building Generational Wealth and Legacy

Wealth Marble

True wealth is not what you leave to your children. True wealth is what you leave in them and what continues to bless others because you once lived.

When Your Wealth Begins to Speak for You

Why This Chapter Matters

If someone asked you today,

"What will remain because you lived?"

How would you answer?

Would you think of your bank account?
Your house?
Your investments?

Or would you think of the people you raised...

The values you lived...

The lives you transformed...
The opportunities you created...
The wisdom you shared...

Every chapter in this book has prepared you for this moment.

You have learned how to:

- Define wealth.
- Develop the right mindset.
- Design your financial future.
- Manage money wisely.
- Build wealth.
- Invest intentionally.
- Create multiple income streams.
- Create value before seeking profit.
- Think entrepreneurially.
- Practice financial wisdom.
- Protect what you build.

Now comes the most important question of all.

What will your wealth build after you're gone?

Because wealth reaches its highest purpose when it continues creating value beyond its owner.
That is legacy.

There was a time when I thought wealth was about reaching a number, a certain income, investment portfolio, and even a certain lifestyle.

But experience has taught me something different.

The greatest achievement is not becoming wealthy. The greatest achievement is becoming the kind of person whose wisdom, values and stewardship continue producing fruit long after you are gone.

Money eventually changes hands. Legacy changes generations.

That is the wealth worth pursuing.

Imagine two families.

The first inherits millions of naira. No one understands budgeting. No one knows how to invest. No one has learned discipline. Within a few years, most of the wealth is gone.

Now imagine another family. The inheritance is modest, but every child understands financial discipline. They know how to create value. They invest consistently. They build businesses. They steward wisely. Generation after generation their wealth grows.

The difference was never the inheritance. The difference was the education.

Money can be transferred in a day. Wisdom is transferred over a lifetime.

What Is Generational Wealth?

Many people believe generational wealth simply means leaving money behind.

That is only part of the story.

Generational wealth is the intentional transfer of financial assets, knowledge, values, opportunities, relationships, and wisdom that enable future generations to flourish.

Money without wisdom disappears.

Wisdom creates more wealth.

The Five Pillars of Generational Wealth

1. Financial Capital

- Money
- Businesses
- Properties
- Investments

These provide opportunity.

But they are only one part of the legacy.

2. Intellectual Capital

- Knowledge
- Skills
- Experience
- Financial education
- The ability to solve problems

Teach your children how wealth is created, not merely how it is spent.

3. Character Capital

- Integrity
- Discipline
- Humility
- Generosity
- Stewardship

Character determines whether wealth survives success.

4. Relational Capital

- Trust
- Family unity
- Mentorship
- Strong networks
- Healthy relationships

Opportunities often travel through relationships.

5. Purpose Capital

- Why does your family exist?
- What values define you?
- What contribution will your family make to society?

Families with purpose build wealth differently.

The Wealth Mentor Blueprint™

The L.E.G.A.C.Y. Framework™

Every lasting legacy is intentionally built using these six principles.

L — Live Your Values

Children imitate what they see more than what they hear.

Your life is your first inheritance.

E — Educate Continuously

Teach financial literacy early.

Talk openly about money.

Explain budgeting.

Explain investing.

Explain generosity.

Financial education should become a family tradition.

G — Grow Together

Build wealth as a family.

Celebrate discipline.

Discuss goals.

Encourage entrepreneurship.

Make wealth creation a shared journey.

A — Accumulate with Purpose

Do not accumulate wealth simply to impress others.

Build assets that strengthen future generations.

Every acquisition should answer the question: "How does this improve our future?"

C — Create Systems

Successful families do not rely on memory.

They build systems.

Document your vision.

Organise important records.

Develop succession plans.

Create structures that continue working even when you are no longer present.

Y — Yield a Lasting Harvest

The ultimate goal is not simply to leave wealth.

It is to leave future generations better equipped to create even greater wealth.

Every generation should become stronger than the one before it.

Framework #1: The Legacy Tree™

ROOTS

- Values
- Character
- Faith
- Integrity

↓

TRUNK

- Knowledge
- Skills
- Financial Wisdom

↓

BRANCHES

- Businesses
- Investments
- Income Streams

↓

FRUIT

- Freedom
- Impact
- Generosity
- Opportunity

↓

SEEDS

- Future Generations

Notice something important; healthy fruit only grows from healthy roots.

Legacy begins below the surface long before it becomes visible.

What Every Family Should Talk About

Many families discuss money only when there is a crisis. Successful families discuss money before there is a need.

Have conversations about:

- Family values.
- Financial goals.
- Entrepreneurship.
- Investing.
- Giving.
- Stewardship.
- Succession.

Silence is not a strategy. Conversation builds continuity.

Framework #2: The Family Legacy Scorecard™

Every year, ask your family these ten questions:

1. Are we creating more value than we consume?
2. Are we living within our means?
3. Are we investing consistently?
4. Are we growing our knowledge?
5. Are we helping one another succeed?
6. Are we giving generously?
7. Are we preparing the next generation?
8. Are we documenting important financial information?
9. Are we strengthening our family values?
10. If this were our final year together, what legacy would remain?

A family's future is shaped by the quality of the questions it consistently asks.

The Greatest Investment

People often ask,

"What is the best investment?"

My answer has changed over the years.

The best investment is not merely the one with the highest financial return.

It is the investment that continues producing value after you are gone.

Sometimes that investment is:

- A child you mentor
- A business you build
- A book you write
- A scholarship you establish
- A principle you teach
- A family you strengthen

Legacy is created every day. Not only at the end of life.

Case Study

Two fathers each leave ₦100 million to their children.

The first father leaves only money. Within a decade, much of it has disappeared through poor decisions and lack of financial discipline.

The second father leaves not only financial assets but also a family constitution, investment principles, regular family financial meetings, mentorship, and a culture of stewardship. Years later, the original wealth has multiplied. The grandchildren are now building businesses, creating employment, and investing wisely.

The difference was not the amount inherited.

The difference was the wisdom transferred.

Wealth Worksheet

My Legacy Blueprint

- The three values I want my family to remember me for: ____
- The financial lessons I want to teach the next generation: ____
- The assets I hope to build: ______________________
- The impact I want my wealth to create: ______________________________________
- The sentence I hope people will honestly say about my life is: _____________________________________

Wealth Checkpoint

☐ Am I building wealth or merely accumulating possessions?

☐ Have I documented my vision?

☐ Am I teaching financial wisdom to those who will come after me?

☐ Does my family understand my values?

☐ If my life ended today, what legacy would continue?

Wealth Challenge

During the next 30 days:

- ✓ Write your Personal Legacy Statement.
- ✓ Schedule one family conversation about money and values.
- ✓ Begin documenting your financial vision.
- ✓ Teach one young person a financial principle.
- ✓ Identify one investment that can benefit future generations.

Remember:

The greatest transfer is not money. The greatest transfer is wisdom.

Money may build a house. Wisdom builds a home.

Money may create comfort. Character creates continuity.

Money may secure one generation. Wisdom can transform many generations.

One day your name will no longer appear on business cards.
One day someone else will occupy your office.
One day your titles will belong to another.

But the values you lived…
The wisdom you shared…
The people you developed…
The opportunities you created…
The legacy you intentionally designed…

will continue speaking long after your voice is silent and that is the highest expression of wealth.

Final Wealth Marble

Your income can end with you. Your impact never has to.

Conclusion

From Income to Impact: The Journey Continues

When you first opened this book, you probably expected to learn about money.

I hope you discovered something much greater.

Money is important.

It provides comfort, creates opportunities, and opens doors that would otherwise remain closed.

But money, by itself, has never been the highest form of wealth.

Throughout these pages, we have journeyed together from defining wealth to understanding the psychology behind financial success; from planning intentionally to managing money wisely; from building assets to investing strategically; from creating multiple streams of income to discovering that lasting wealth is created by first creating value. We explored entrepreneurship, stewardship, preservation, and finally, the responsibility of building a legacy that outlives us.

If there is one lesson I hope remains with you long after you close this book, it is this:

Wealth is never an accident, it is intentionally designed.

Every financial decision you make today is quietly shaping the life you will live tomorrow.

Every naira you spend, save, invest, or give is writing a story.

The question is not whether you are building wealth.

The question is: What kind of wealth are you building?

Will it disappear with you or will it continue creating opportunities, transforming lives, and strengthening generations long after you are gone?

True wealth is never measured solely by the size of your income, your investment portfolio, or your net worth.

It is measured by the problems you solve, the value you create, the opportunities you open for others, the wisdom you transfer, and the legacy you leave behind.

I have spent much of my life working alongside individuals, businesses, entrepreneurs, and institutions making financial decisions that shaped futures. Those experiences convinced me that the greatest limitation facing many people is not a lack of opportunity.

It is a lack of financial direction.

Knowledge changes that. Discipline sustains it. Purpose gives it meaning.

As you leave these pages, I encourage you not to admire these principles. Apply them.

Do not merely earn more, become more valuable.

Do not merely accumulate more, steward more wisely.

Do not merely pursue success, pursue significance.

- Design a financial plan.

- Invest consistently.
- Create value relentlessly.
- Protect what you build.
- Teach your children.
- Mentor others.
- Create opportunities.

Leave systems that continue serving people long after your work is done.

Remember that wealth reaches its highest purpose when it becomes a tool for transformation.

When one person becomes financially wise, a family becomes stronger.

When families become stronger, communities flourish.

When communities flourish, nations prosper.

That is why financial wisdom is not merely a personal advantage; it is a national asset.

As I bring this book to a close, I leave you with one final challenge.

Do not ask yourself,

"How much money do I want to make?"

Ask yourself,

"What kind of life do I want my wealth to make possible?"

That single question has the power to change every financial decision you make from this day forward.

One day, your bank account will become history. Your possessions will belong to someone else. Your career will eventually end.

But your impact...

Your values...

Your wisdom...

The lives you transformed...

The opportunities you created...

The legacy you designed...

Those will continue speaking long after you are gone.

May you choose to build the kind of wealth that time cannot erase.

May you intentionally move... From Income to Impact.

The journey does not end here.

In many ways, it has only just begun.

"The greatest measure of wealth is not what you leave for people. It is what you leave in people."

Augusta Olachi Anyanwu-Egbom
Author. Wealth Mentor. Nation Builder.

...Continue the Journey

Thank you for reading Wealth by Design.

To access bonus resources, downloadable tools, updates, and connect with the Wealth Mentor community, visit: www.tdicfoundation.org/wealthbydesign

Follow Augusta Olachi Anyanwu-Egbom on FB, In, X for more insights on wealth creation, leadership, and legacy.

Dedicated Social Media Pages:

Wealth Mentor

Wealthmentor_1

Wealth Mentor

Tel: +2348023319710 / +447480539285

www.ingramcontent.com/pod-product-compliance
Lightning Source LLC
LaVergne TN
LVHW041208061126
851857LV00018B/1981
* 9 7 8 9 7 8 6 8 9 7 5 2 3 *